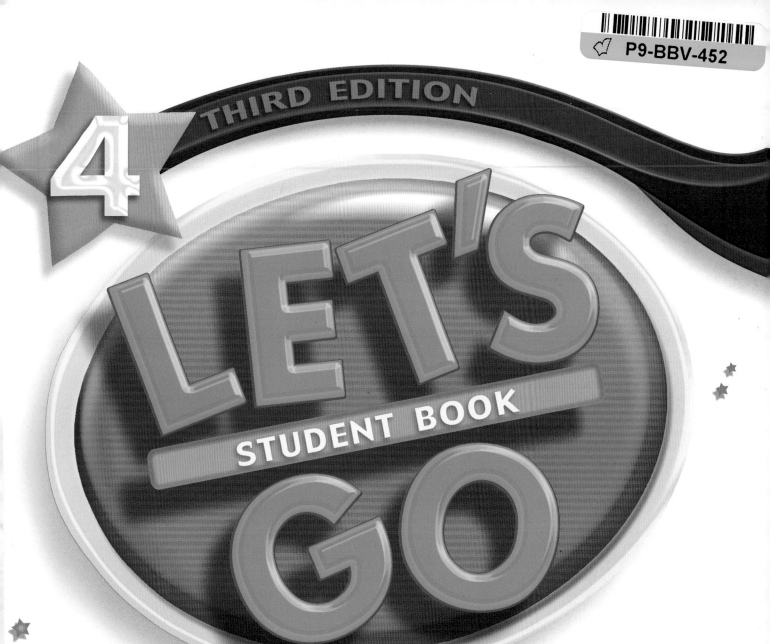

THIRD EDITION

4

LET'S GO

STUDENT BOOK

Ritsuko Nakata

Karen Frazier

Barbara Hoskins

with grammar chants by Carolyn Graham

OXFORD

UNIVERSITY PRESS

OXFORD
UNIVERSITY PRESS

198 Madison Avenue
New York, NY 10016 USA

Great Clarendon Street, Oxford ox2 6dp UK

Oxford University Press is a department of the University of Oxford.
It furthers the University's objective of excellence in research, scholarship,
and education by publishing worldwide in

Oxford New York

Auckland Cape Town Dar es Salaam Hong Kong Karachi
Kuala Lumpur Madrid Melbourne Mexico City Nairobi
New Delhi Shanghai Taipei Toronto

With offices in

Argentina Austria Brazil Chile Czech Republic France Greece
Guatemala Hungary Italy Japan Poland Portugal Singapore
South Korea Switzerland Thailand Turkey Ukraine Vietnam

OXFORD and OXFORD ENGLISH are registered trademarks of
Oxford University Press

Senior Editor: Paul Phillips
Editor: Joseph McGasko
Art Director: Maj-Britt Hagsted
Design Project Manager: Amelia L. Carling
Designers: Mia Gomez, Sangeeta E. Ramcharan, Alicia Dorn (cover)
Art Editor: Justine Eun
Production Manager: Shanta Persaud
Production Controller: Eve Wong

Student Book:
ISBN 978 0 19 439428 4

Student Book with CD-ROM:
ISBN 978 0 19 439435 2

Student Book as pack component:
ISBN 978 0 19 439442 0

CD-ROM as pack component:
ISBN 978 0 19 439560 1

Printed in China.

10 9 8 7 6

This book is printed on paper from certified and well-managed sources.

Acknowledgments

Illustrators: COVER: Zina Saunders, Janet Skiles; INTERIOR: David Benham/
Graham-Cameron Illustration: 7, 16, 43, 52, 61; Kevin Brown: 14, 29, 34; Mircea
Catusanu/Painted-Words, Inc.: 7, 17, 31, 48, 70; Ruth Flanigan: 4, 12, 18, 23, 41, 48,
54, 68; Patrick Girouard/Portfolio Solutions: 5, 15, 22, 36, 40, 54, 60, 66, 72; Steve
Henry/Cornell & McCarthy: 18, 30, 59; Richard Hoit/Deborah Wolfe: 9, 22, 39, 63;
Chris Lench/Liz Sanders Agency: 34; Anthony Lewis/HK Portfolio: 11, 14, 18, 24, 42,
67, 72; Janet McDonnell: 6, 21, 32, 40, 47, 57, 69; John Nez/The Herman Agency: 11,
25, 45, 49, 51, 65; Vilma Ortiz-Dillon: 53; Marilee Herrald-Pilz/Storybook Artists:
44; Chris Reed: 8, 26, 36, 43, 66, 71; Dana Regan/Portfolio Solutions: 6, 21, 27, 39,
54, 58, 65, 72; Zina Saunders: 2, 10, 20, 28, 38, 46, 47, 56, 64; Jane Smith: 12, 18, 30,
45, 50; Mark Stephens/Maggie Byer-Sprinzeles: 29, 57; Mike Wesley/Painted-Words,
Inc.: 4, 13, 24, 33, 51, 62; Necdet Yilmaz/Wendy Lynn & Co.: 19, 37, 55, 73.

Photo Credits: Ardea: Hans Judy Beste, 45 (koala); Bill Coster, 35 (swan); John
Daniels, 35 (falcon); Francois Gohier, 35 (whale); Tom Pat Leeson, 35 (duck); The
Image Works: Tony Savino, 37 (log flume); Jupiter Unlimited: Ablestock.com, 19
(Pyramids); Comstock.com, 35 (horse); Minden Pictures: Norbert Wu, 35 (sailfish);
SuperStock: age footstock, 19 (Mayan ruins), 35 (lion, cheetah), 45 (kangaroo,
crocodile); Angelo Cavalli, 37 (Iguazu Falls); Dynamic Graphics Value, 55 (Grand
Canyon); Pixtal, 19 (Louvre pyramid); SuperStock, Inc., 55 (Carlsbad Caverns);
Donald Tipton, 35 (dolphin); Steve Vidler, 37 (Niagara Falls), 55 (jungle cave).

Table of Contents

Hi, I'm Ginger!

Hi, I'm Sam!

Let's Start

Let's Learn

Let's Learn More

Let's Build

Let's Read

Units Review

Let's Read About

Let's Read About

Let's Start

A. Let's talk. CD 1 02

What's the date today?

It's the 21st.

Oh! Today's my aunt's birthday.

Really? Yesterday was my father's birthday.

When's your birthday?

It's on August 3rd. When is your birthday?

My birthday was three weeks ago.

I didn't know that! Happy birthday!

B. Let's practice. CD 1 03

When's your birthday?
It's on August 3rd.

C. Practice the sentences. Ask and answer. CD 1 04 CD 1 05

> **What's the date today?**
>   It's the 21st.
> **What was the date yesterday?**
>   It was the 20th.
> **What's the date going to be tomorrow?**
>   It's going to be the 22nd.

January

February
S	M	T	W	T	F	S
				1	2	3	4
5	6	7	8	9	10	11
12	13	14	15	16	17	18
19	20	21	22	23	24	25
26	27	28

March
S	M	T	W	T	F	S
				1	2	3	4
5	6	7	8	10	10	11
12	13	14	15	16	17	18
19	20	21	22	23	24	25
26	27	28	29	30	31

April
S	M	T	W	T	F	S
						1
2	3	4	5	6	7	8
9	10	11	12	13	14	15
16	17	18	19	20	21	22
23 30	24	25	26	27	28	29

January
Sunday	Monday	Tuesday	Wednesday	Thursday	Friday	Saturday
1 1st	2 2nd	3 3rd	4 4th	5 5th	6 6th	7 7th
8 8th	9 9th	10 10th	11 11th	12 12th	13 13th	14 14th
15 15th	16 16th	17 17th	18 18th	19 19th	20 20th	21 Today! 21st
22 22nd	23 23rd	24 24th	25 25th	26 26th	27 27th	28 28th
29 29th	30 30th	31 31st				

December
S	M	T	W	T	F	S
1	2	3	4
5	6	7	8	9	10	11
12	13	14	15	16	17	18
19	20	21	22	23	24	25
26	27	28	29	30	31

November
S	M	T	W	T	F	S
			1	2	3	4	5	6
7	8	9	10	11	12	13
14	15	16	17	18	19	20
21	22	23	24	25	26	27
28	29	30

October
S	M	T	W	T	F	S
					1	2
3	4	5	6	7	8	9
10	11	12	13	14	15	16
17	18	19	20	21	22	23
24 31	25	26	27	28	29	30

May
S	M	T	W	T	F	S
	1	2	3	4	5	6
7	8	10	10	11	12	13
14	15	16	17	18	19	20
21	22	23	24	25	26	27
28	29	30	31

June
S	M	T	W	T	F	S
				1	2	3
4	5	6	7	8	9	10
11	12	13	14	15	16	17
18	19	20	21	22	23	24
25	26	27	28	29	30

July
S	M	T	W	T	F	S
						1
2	3	4	5	6	7	8
9	10	11	12	13	14	15
16	19	20	21	22	23	24
25	26	27	28	29	30	31

August
S	M	T	W	T	F	S
1	2	3	4	5	6	7
8	9	10	11	12	12	14
15	16	17	18	19	20	21
22	23	24	25	26	27	28
29	30	31

September
S	M	T	W	T	F	S
				1	2	3	4
5	6	7	8	9	10	11
12	13	14	15	16	17	18
19	20	21	22	23	24	25
26	27	28	29	30

Did You Know?

What's the date?
  It's the 15th.
  It's May 15th.
  It's Tuesday, May 15th.

Let's Learn

A. Practice the words. CD 1 06

1. took a test

2. had a party

3. flew a kite

4. went to the store

5. met a movie star

6. drank hot chocolate

B. Practice the sentences. CD 1 07 CD 1 08 CD 1 09

He She	had a party yesterday.
He She	didn't drink hot chocolate yesterday.

take	→	took
have	→	had
fly	→	flew
go	→	went
meet	→	met
drink	→	drank

1. 2. 3. 4. 5. 6.

C. Practice the question and answer.

What did	he	do yesterday?
	she	
He	took a test.	
She		

D. Ask and answer.

Did	he	fly a kite yesterday?			
	she				
	Yes,	he	did.	No, he	didn't.
		she		she	

Let's Learn More

What happened?

He ate too much chocolate.

A. Practice the words.

CD 1 13

1. ate too much chocolate

2. broke a window

3. got a present

4. found some money

5. lost his cell phone

6. won a race

B. Practice the sentences.

CD 1 14   CD 1 15   CD 1 16

He She They	won a race.
He She They	didn't find any money.

eat	→	ate
break	→	broke
get	→	got
find	→	found
lose	→	lost
win	→	won

1.

2.

3.

C. Practice the question and answer.

What happened?	He	found some money.
	She	
	They	

D. Practice the grammar chant.

When's your birthday?

    It was the day before yesterday.

What did you do?

    I had a party.

What happened?

    We had a race.

Did you win?

        Yes, I won. I came in 1st place!

Let's Build

A. Make sentences. CD 1 20

> I met a movie star **on the** 13th.

August

S	M	T	W	T	F	S
			1	2	3	4	5
6	7	8	9	10	11	12
13	14	15	16	17	18	19
20	21	22	23	24	25	26
27	28	29	30	31		

1. lost my music player
2. found my music player
3. met a movie star
4. ate at a restaurant
5. flew a kite
6. had a party

B. Ask and answer. CD 1 21

> When did he **fly a kite**?
> He **flew a kite on** Sunday the 20th.

Let's Read

A. Read. CD 1 22

Welcome to Abby's Page

My birthday was great this year. First, my parents and I went to a restaurant for breakfast. I had birthday candles on my pancakes! Then, we went to the Space Center. I took a tour and met an astronaut. It was a lot of fun!

go	→	went
have	→	had
take	→	took

New Words

parents
candles
Space Center
tour
astronaut

B. Answer the questions.

1. How was Abby's birthday this year?
2. Did she eat breakfast at home?
3. Who did she meet at the Space Center?

C. Choose the sentence with the same meaning.

My parents and I went to the Space Center.

1. I went to the Space Center.
2. We went to the Space Center.
3. They went to the Space Center.

Let's Start

A. Let's talk. CD 1 23

> The school trip is tomorrow. I'm really excited!
>
> Me, too!

> What's the weather going to be like?
>
> It's going to be cold.

> Should we take our jackets?
>
> Yes, we should.

> Should we take our umbrellas?
>
> No, I don't think so. It isn't going to rain.

B. Let's practice. CD 1 24

The school trip is tomorrow. I'm really excited!
Me, too!

C. Practice the words. Ask and answer.

1. cool

2. cold

3. warm

4. hot

5. foggy

6. humid

> What's the weather going to be like tomorrow?
> It's going to be cold.

D. Practice the grammar chant.

What's the weather going to be like tomorrow?
The newspaper says it's going to snow.
Do you think we should take our umbrellas?
I'm not the weatherman. I don't know!

Let's Learn

A. Practice the words. (CD 1 28)

1. a towel

2. a hat

3. a swimsuit

4. a tent

5. a flashlight

6. a sleeping bag

7. sunglasses

8. sunscreen

B. Say these. (CD 1 29)

He's going to go to the mountains.

She's going to go to the beach.

C. Practice the sentences. (CD 1 30) (CD 1 31)

| He She | should take sunscreen. | He She | shouldn't take a tent. |

D. Practice the question and answer.

Should	he she they	take sunscreen?

Yes,	he she they	should.	No,	he she they	shouldn't.

> shouldn't =
> should not

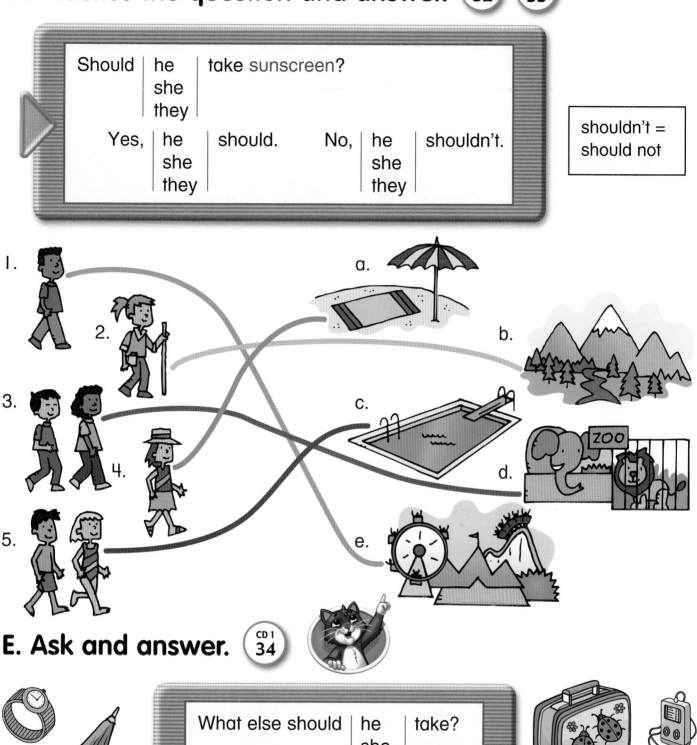

1.

2.

3.

4.

5.

a.

b.

c.

d.

e.

E. Ask and answer.

What else should	he she they	take?

He She They	should take a camera.

Let's Learn More

What's she going to do?

She's probably going to play tennis.

A. Practice the words.
 CD 1 35

1. a mitt 2. a bat 3. a bicycle 4. a helmet

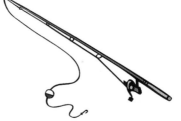

5. a tennis ball 6. a tennis racket 7. a fishing rod 8. a bucket

B. Practice the sentences.
 CD 1 36   CD 1 37

> He has a mitt and a bat.
> He doesn't have a fishing rod or a bucket.
> He's probably going to play baseball.

1.

2.

3.

4.

C. Practice the question and answer. 38 39

What's | he / she | going to do?

He's / She's | probably going to go hiking.

What are they going to do?
They're probably going to play baseball.

play baseball
play tennis
ride a bicycle
go fishing
go hiking
go swimming

1.

2.

3.

4.

5.

6.

Did You Know?

He's going to eat. = 100% sure
He's probably going to eat. = not 100% sure

Let's Build

A. Make sentences. CD 1 40

He has a towel. He's probably going to go to the pool.
She wants a cat. She's probably going to go to the pet store.

They have a kite. They're probably going to go to the park.

Bookstore | Restaurant | Pet Store | LIBRARY | Bakery | SWIMMING POOL | PARK

1   2   3   4   5   6

B. Ask and answer. CD 1 41

| Where's | he / she | going to go? |

| He's / She's | probably going to go to the library. |

Where are they going to go?
They're probably going to go to the park.

Let's Read

A. Read. CD 1 42

How to Make a Rainbow

Do you like rainbows? You can make a rainbow indoors.

First, put water in a glass.

Second, put a small mirror inside the glass and tilt it up slightly.

Third, turn off the lights.

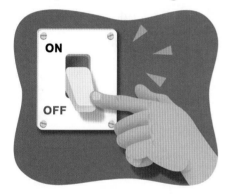

Shine a flashlight onto the mirror. You're going to see a rainbow on the wall!

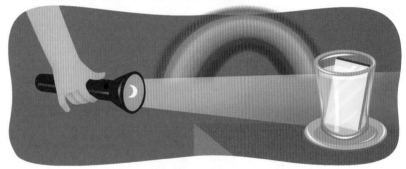

B. Answer the questions.

1. Can you make a rainbow?
2. What should you do first?
3. Where are you going to see a rainbow?

New Words	
a rainbow	tilt it up slightly
indoors	turn off the lights
mirror	shine

C. Choose the correct picture.

Which picture shows the meaning of *tilt it up slightly*?

a. 　　b. 　　c.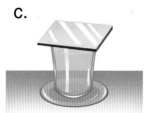

Units 1-2 Listen and Review

A. Listen and write. CD 1 43

SUNDAY	MONDAY	TUESDAY	WEDNESDAY	THURSDAY	FRIDAY	SATURDAY
	TODAY					
___	___	___	___	___	___	___

B. Listen and circle. CD 1 44

1.   a   b   c
2.   a   b   c
3.   a   b   c
4.   a   b   c
5.   a   b   c
6.   a   b   c

CHRIS AND CiNDY'S TREASURE HUNT

Part One

A. Read. CD 1 45

"We're going to go on a treasure hunt," said Aunt Angie. "We're going to take my airplane."
"Yeah!" said Chris and Cindy.

Aunt Angie had the first clue for the treasure hunt. Chris and Cindy read it.

New Words

treasure hunt
clue
sand
holding

It's not a beach, but there's a lot of sand. You should take your hats and sunscreen. Uncle Al is holding your next clue in front of a big triangle.

"I think I know!" said Cindy.

B. Where are they going to go next?

a.

b.

c.

Let's Start

A. Let's talk. CD 1 46

What do you want to be?

I want to be an astronaut.

Wow, that's great.

Do you want to be an astronaut, too?

No, I don't. I want to be a singer.

What about you, Scott?

I want to be rich!

B. Let's practice. CD 1 47

What do you want to be?
I want to be an astronaut.

C. Practice the words. Ask and answer.

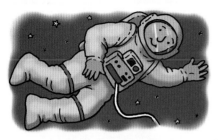

1. an astronaut

2. a singer

3. a musician

4. a news reporter

5. a writer

6. a scientist

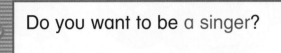

Do you want to be a singer?   Yes, I do.
No, I don't.

D. Practice the grammar chant.

What do you want to be?
  I want to be a dancer.
  What about you?
I want to be a singer.
  Great idea!
  Come on, let's go.
  We can sing and dance
    on a TV show!

Let's Learn

Does he want to be a pop idol?

Yes, he does.

A. Practice the words.

CD 1 51

1. a flight attendant

2. a pop idol

3. a truck driver

4. an architect

5. a tour guide

6. a delivery person

B. Practice the sentences.

CD 1 52   CD 1 53

He She	wants to be a flight attendant.
He She	doesn't want to be a delivery person.

1.

2.

3.

C. Practice the question and answer. CD 1 54 CD 1 55

| What does | he
she | want to be? | He
She | wants to be a truck driver. |

D. Ask and answer. CD 1 56

| Does | he
she | want to be a delivery person? |

| Yes, | he
she | does. | No, | he
she | doesn't. |

Let's Learn More

 What does she want to do?

She wants to sail a boat.

A. Practice the words. (CD 1 57)

1. climb a mountain

2. build a house

3. sail a boat

4. travel around the world

5. design a video game

6. drive a car

B. Practice the sentences. (CD 1 58) (CD 1 59)

He She	wants to drive a car.
He She	doesn't want to travel around the world.

1.

2.

3.

C. Practice the question and answer.

> | What does | he | want to do? |
> |---|---|---|
> | | she | |
>
> | He | wants to design a video game. |
> |---|---|
> | She | |

D. Ask and answer.

> | Does | he | want to build a house? |
> |---|---|---|
> | | she | |
>
> | Yes, | he | does. | No, | he | doesn't. |
> |---|---|---|---|---|---|
> | | she | | | she | |

E. What about you?

What do you want to do?

Let's Build

Play the game. Make sentences. (CD 1 63)

I want to _____, but I don't want to _____.

Start

| study English | talk on the telephone | swim |
| speak English | watch TV | run |

play Ping-Pong
play baseball

use chopsticks
do a magic trick

| walk the dog | ride a bicycle |
| feed the turtle | drive a car |

sing
dance

| eat an apple | do homework | cook dinner |
| drink hot chocolate | listen to music | make breakfast |

take pictures
take a bath

Finish

Let's Read

A. Read. CD 1 64

Anna and Teri Johnson, Volunteer Sisters

Anna Johnson is a volunteer at the zoo. She likes to work with animals. She works with dolphins every day. She feeds them every morning and helps train them, too. Someday Anna wants to be a dolphin trainer.

Teri is Anna's sister. She is a volunteer at the hospital. She doesn't want to work with animals. She likes to help people. She wants to be a nurse someday.

B. Answer the questions.

1. What is Anna doing at the zoo?
2. Does she like to work with animals?
3. What does Teri want to be?

New Words

volunteer	trainer
dolphins	hospital

C. Choose the correct answer.

What does a dolphin trainer do?

a. rides on a train with dolphins
b. drives a train with dolphins
c. works with dolphins

Let's Start

A. Let's talk. CD 1 65

What's your favorite subject?

I like science.

Why do you like it?

I think it's easy.

I don't think so. I think it's hard.

Which subject do you like best?

I like English. It's easier than science.

I like English, too.

B. Let's practice. CD 1 66

Why do you like science?
I think it's easy.

C. Practice the words. Ask and answer.

1. history

2. science

3. English

4. P.E. (physical education)

5. geography

6. literature

> What's your favorite subject?
> I like history.

D. Practice the grammar chant.

What's your favorite subject?
   I like P.E.
Why do you like it?
   No homework!
   What about you?
I like science.
   Why do you like it?
Nice teacher!

E. What about you?

What's your favorite subject?

Let's Learn

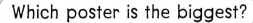

Which poster is the biggest?

The blue poster is the biggest.

A. Practice the words. CD 1 70

1.

bottle / bottles

2.

box / boxes

3.

bag / bags

B. Practice the sentences. CD 1 71 CD 1 72

The orange bottle **is bigger** than the blue bottle.
The green bottle **is the** biggest.

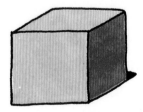
big

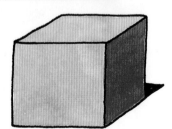
bigger

biggest

small

smaller

smallest

30 Unit 4 / School

C. Practice the questions and answers. CD 1 73 CD 1 74 CD 1 75

Which pencil is the longest?
   The yellow pencil is the longest.
Which pencil is the shortest?
   The red pencil is the shortest.

big	→ bigger	→ the biggest
small	→ smaller	→ the smallest
long	→ longer	→ the longest
short	→ shorter	→ the shortest
heavy	→ heavier	→ the heaviest
light	→ lighter	→ the lightest

1. heavy / light

2. long / short

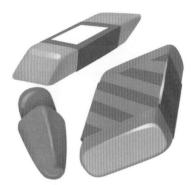

3. big / small

4. light / heavy

5. short / long

6. small / big

D. Ask and answer. CD 1 76

Is the blue pencil the longest?
   Yes, it is.   No, it isn't.

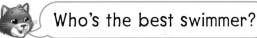

Who's the best swimmer?

She's the best!

Let's Learn More

A. Practice the words. CD 1 77

1. good — Matt

2. better — Lisa

3. the best — Keith

4. bad — Beth

5. worse — Jim

6. the worst — Wendy

B. Practice the sentence. CD 1 78 CD 1 79

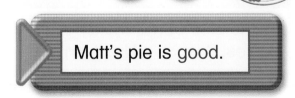

Matt's pie is good.

C. Practice the questions and answers.

Who's the	best	swimmer?	Ryan is the best.
	worst		Kevin is the worst.

 = Ryan   = Ann   = Kevin

1. swimmer

2. dancer

3. singer

4. runner

5. soccer player

6. cook

D. Ask and answer.

Is Kevin a better runner than Ann?	Is Kevin the best swimmer?
Yes, he is. No, he isn't.	Yes, he is. No, he isn't.

Let's Build

A. Make sentences. CD 1 83

> The police car is heavier than the motorcycle.
> The fire engine is the heaviest.

heavy	light	big	long

1. motorcycle
   police car
   fire engine

2. paper
   pencil
   paper clip

3. hairbrush
   key
   coin

4. ruler
   jump rope
   ribbon

B. Practice the grammar chant. CD 1 84

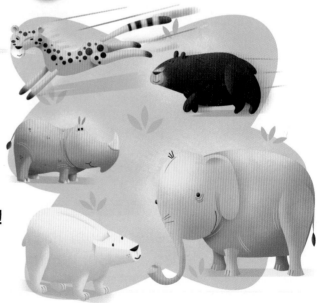

Bears can run.
Lions run faster.
But cheetahs are the fastest of them all!

Don't ever race with a cheetah.
Cheetahs are the fastest of them all!

Rhinos are big.
Polar bears are bigger.
But elephants are the biggest of them all!

Don't ever fight with an elephant.
Elephants are the biggest of them all!

Let's Read

A. Read.  CD 1 85

Which One Is the Fastest?

Some animals are fast and some are slow. Some animals move only on land and some move only in water. Other animals move in the air. Let's look at the speed of some animals.

1. Which animal is the fastest on land?

a. a lion

b. a cheetah

c. a horse

2. Which animal is the fastest in the air?

a. a swan

b. a duck

c. a falcon

3. Which animal is the fastest in water?

a. a sailfish

b. a dolphin

c. a whale

Animal	Speed (kph)
falcon	320
swan	90
duck	85
cheetah	112
lion	80
horse	76
sailfish	109
whale	54
dolphin	40

New Words

on land	falcon
in water	sailfish
in the air	whale
swan	

Answers to Quiz: 1. b. 2. c. 3. a.

B. Do you know?

1. Which three animals are the fastest?
2. Which animal is the fastest of all?
3. Which animal is the slowest in water?

C. Choose the correct answer.

Where does a dolphin live?

1. in water   2. on water   3. by water

Units 3-4 Listen and Review

A. Listen and circle. CD 1 86

1.

2.

3.

4.

B. Listen and check. CD 1 87

1.

2.

3.

4.

Nina   Jill   John

CHRIS AND CINDY'S TREASURE HUNT

Part Two

A. Read. CD 1 88

"Egypt is hot!" said Chris.

"Look," said Cindy. "There's the Great Pyramid."

"And there's Uncle Al with three water bottles!" said Chris.

"Hi, kids!" he said.

"Hi, Uncle Al. Do you have our next clue?" asked Cindy.

"Yes, I do," he said. "Here it is."

New Words

Egypt
Great Pyramid
kids
waterfall

Find the biggest waterfall and ride a boat in front of it.

"This clue is harder," said Cindy. "But I think I know," said Chris.

B. Where are they going to go next?

a.

b.

c.

Let's Start

A. Let's talk. CD 2 02

B. Let's practice. CD 2 03

| Can you wait for us? | Sure, no problem! |
| | Sorry, I can't. |

C. Practice the words and sentences.

1. worried

2. surprised

3. interested

4. excited

5. bored

6. embarrassed

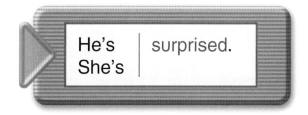

He's
She's | surprised.

D. Practice the grammar chant.

He's very worried.
So is she.
She's excited.
So are we.
We're surprised.
So are they.
Our teacher gave
  a test today.

Let's Learn

 What did he do yesterday?

He played a board game.

A. Practice the words. CD 2 07

1. watched a baseball game

2. practiced the violin

3. downloaded music

4. listened to the radio

5. played a board game

6. visited their grandparents

B. Practice the sentences. CD 2 08 CD 2 09

He She	practiced the violin.
He She	didn't download music.

1.

2.

3.

C. Practice the questions and answers.

| What did | he | do yesterday? | He | practiced the violin. |
| | she | | She | |

| What did they do yesterday? | They visited their grandparents. |

1.

2.

3.

4.

D. Ask and answer.

CD 2 12

| Did | he | listen to the radio? |
| | she | |

| Yes, | he | did. | No, | he | didn't. |
| | she | | | she | |

Did they play a board game?
   Yes, they did.   No, they didn't.

E. What about you?

What did you do this morning? What did you do yesterday?

Let's Learn More

Where did he go?

He went down a hill.

A. Say these. CD 2 13

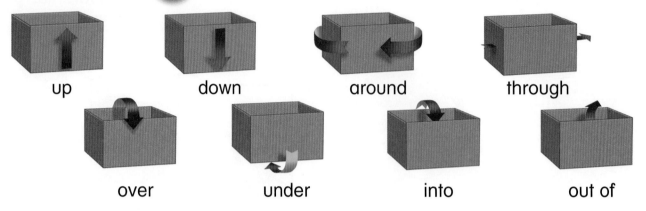

up   down   around   through

over   under   into   out of

B. Practice the words. CD 2 14

1.

under a bridge   up a hill

2.

into the woods   out of the woods

3.

around a pond   over a bridge

4.

through a tunnel   down a hill

C. Practice the sentence. CD 2 15 CD 2 16

| He She They | went under a bridge **and** up a hill. |

D. Practice the question and answer.

| Where did the | boy | go? | He went over the wall. |
| | girl | | She went over the tunnel. |

E. Where did the cat and dog go?

Let's Build

A. Answer the questions. CD 2 20

Where did Ken go?
Who did he go with?
What did he do?
What did he eat?
When did he go?

Where did Stacy go?
Who did she go with?
What did she do?
What did she eat?
When did she go?

Ken

Steve

March 13th

Lori

Stacy

February 22nd

B. What about you?

1. Where did you go for your summer vacation?
2. Who did you go with?
3. What did you do?
4. What did you eat?
5. When did you go?

Word Box

amusement park
ride a roller coaster
french fries
museum
sandwich
look at pictures

Let's Read

A. Read. CD 2 21

Aunt Tina's Trip

Dear Joey,

We are having fun in Australia! Uncle Mark and I went to the wildlife park yesterday. I fed a kangaroo and held a koala. Uncle Mark went through the reptile house and fed a crocodile. He looked scared! Tomorrow we are going to go sailing.

See you soon!
Aunt Tina

Joey Johnson
21 Maple Road
Rockview, MN 12345

New Words

Australia
wildlife park
kangaroo
koala
reptile
crocodile

B. Answer the questions.

| feed | → | fed |
| hold | → | held |

1. Where are Aunt Tina and Uncle Mark?
2. Who fed a kangaroo?
3. Where are they going to go tomorrow?

C. Choose the correct picture.

Which picture shows the meaning of *He looked scared*?

a.

b.

c.

Let's Start

A. Let's talk. (CD 2 / 22)

Can I help you?

Yes, thanks. I'm looking for someone.

Who are you looking for?

I'm looking for my aunt.

What does she look like?

She has short red hair and green eyes.

Is that her over there?

Yes, it is. Thanks!

B. Let's practice. (CD 2 / 23)

Can I help you?
Yes, thanks.
No, thanks. I'm OK.

Did You Know?

The word *one* in *someone* means *person* or *people*.

someone = one person
no one = no people
everyone = all people

C. Practice the words. Ask and answer.

Kate

 1. aunt

 2. uncle

 3. cousin

 4. younger sister

 5. mom

 6. dad

 7. grandma

 8. grandpa

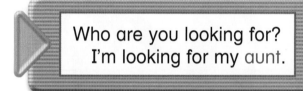

> Who are you looking for?
> I'm looking for my aunt.

mom = mother
dad = father
grandma = grandmother
grandpa = grandfather

D. Practice the grammar chant.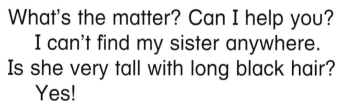

What's the matter? Can I help you?
    I can't find my sister anywhere.
Is she very tall with long black hair?
    Yes!
Look! She's right over there.
    That's my sister. What a surprise.
    Long black hair and beautiful eyes!

Unit 6 / People **47**

What does she look like?

She has curly hair.

Let's Learn

A. Practice the words. CD 2 27

Hair Color
brown hair
black hair
blond hair
red hair
gray hair

Hair Style
curly hair
long hair
straight hair
a ponytail
bangs

Face
a moustache
a beard

Eye Color
black eyes
brown eyes
blue eyes
green eyes

B. Practice the sentence. CD 2 28 CD 2 29

He
She | has short red hair **and** green eyes.

1. 2. 3. 4. 5. 6. 7. 8.

C. Practice the question and answer. CD 2 30 CD 2 31

> **What does** his cousin **look like?**
> His cousin **has** brown hair **and** blue eyes.

1. cousin

2. friend

3. older sister

4. younger brother

5. aunt

6. uncle

7. grandma

8. grandpa

9. mom

10. dad

D. What about you?

1. What do you look like?
2. What does your cousin look like?
3. What does your friend look like?

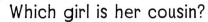
Let's Learn More

A. Practice the words. CD 2 32

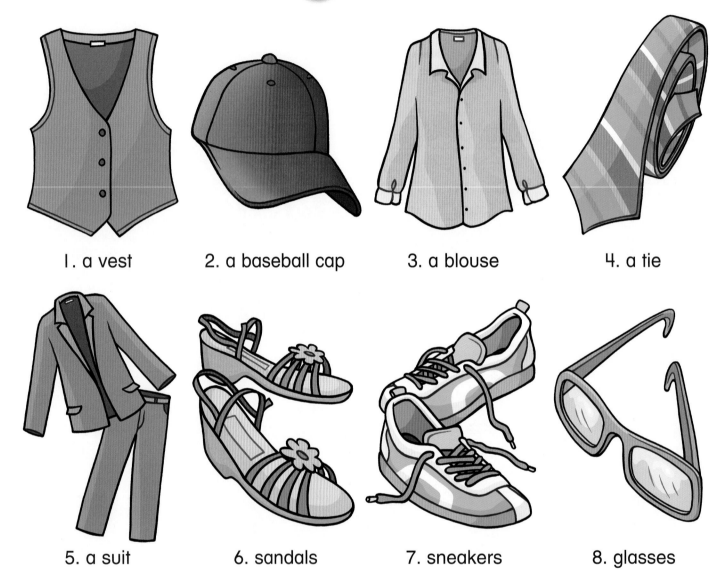

1. a vest
2. a baseball cap
3. a blouse
4. a tie

5. a suit
6. sandals
7. sneakers
8. glasses

B. Practice the sentences. CD 2 33 CD 2 34

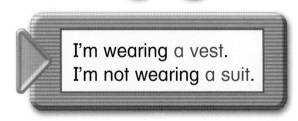

I'm wearing a vest.
I'm not wearing a suit.

C. Practice the question and answer. CD 2 35 CD 2 36

> Which boy is Brian's older brother?
> He's the boy with curly brown hair and brown eyes.
> He's the boy in shorts and a blue, striped shirt.

1. older brother
2. older sister
3. mom
4. uncle
5. dad
6. grandpa
7. aunt
8. grandma
9. younger brother

man
woman
boy
girl

D. Practice the grammar chant. CD 2 37

Is that Jim's older brother there,
the boy in shorts with the curly hair?
   No, Jim's brother is wearing jeans
   and a long purple T-shirt from New Orleans.

Let's Build

A. Look and answer the questions.

CD 2
38

1. Anna is the girl in the red shorts and white T-shirt.

   She's the girl with a long, black ponytail and bangs.

   Where's Anna?

2. Alex is the boy with short, curly brown hair and brown eyes.

   He's in the red sneakers and yellow T-shirt.

   Where's Alex?

3. Emily is the woman in the gray suit and white blouse.

   She's the woman with short blond hair and blue eyes.

   Where's Emily?

4. Sam is the man in the black jeans and glasses.

   He's the man with a moustache and green eyes.

   Where's Sam?

B. Answer the questions.

CD 2
39

1. What is Anna doing?
2. Who is Alex with?

3. What is Emily eating?
4. Where is Sam going to go?

Let's Read

A. Read. (CD 2 40)

Let's make a fingerprint. First, put lotion on your hands. Then, touch a mirror.

Put powder on the mirror. Brush the powder away. You should see a fingerprint.

Put a piece of tape on the fingerprint. Lift the tape and put it on a piece of black paper. Do this for every finger. Then you can see all of your fingerprints. Every fingerprint is different!

New Words

fingerprint
lotion
powder
a piece of tape
lift

B. Answer the questions.

1. Where can you find your fingerprints?
2. Where do you put the powder?
3. Are all fingerprints the same?

C. Choose the best title.

1. My Fingerprint Is Different
2. You Should Look at Fingerprints
3. Let's Make Fingerprints

A. Listen and circle. CD 2 41

1.

(a) (b) (c)

2.

(a) (b) (c)

3.

(a) (b) (c)

4.

(a) (b) (c)

B. Listen and number. CD 2 42

Alice's father ☐

Alice's mother ☐

Alice's grandmother ☐

Alice ☐

Alice's sister ☐

Alice's cousin ☐

CHRIS AND CINDY'S TREASURE HUNT

Part Three

A. Read. (CD 2 43)

"Iguazu Falls is beautiful!" said Cindy.

"But I'm wet!" said Chris.

"Are you Chris and Cindy?" asked a man.

"Yes, we are!"

"Here's your clue," said the man.

This place is in the desert, but it's always cold. It's underground and dark. Find your treasure near the castle in the Big Room.

New Words

Iguazu Falls
wet
desert
underground
castle
cave

"There are a lot of deserts in the world," said Chris.

"But this is a desert with a big cave," said Cindy. "I think I know."

B. Where are they going to go next?

a.

b.

c.

Let's Start

A. Let's talk. (CD 2 44)

Are you going to do anything this weekend?

Yes, I am. I'm going to see my cousin.

How old is your cousin?

He's 14. He's my favorite cousin.

What about you? What are you going to do?

I'm going to play ice hockey. I have a game tomorrow.

Good luck! I hope you win.

Thanks!

B. Let's practice. (CD 2 45)

Are you going to do anything this weekend?
Yes, I am. I'm going to see my cousin.
No, I'm not. I'm going to stay home.

C. Practice the words. Ask and answer.

1. go shopping

2. plant flowers

3. play ice hockey

4. see a play

5. go horseback riding

6. play softball

What's	he she	going to do?	He's She's	going to go shopping.
What are they going to do?			They're going to play ice hockey.	

D. Practice the grammar chant. CD 2 48

What are you going to do this weekend?
   I'm going to go shopping.
What are you going to buy?
   I'm going to buy skis.
Skis? Why?
It's not going to snow.
   I know. I know.
   No mountains here. No hills, no snow.
Where are you going to ski?
   I don't know!

Let's Learn

 When's he going to go backpacking?

He's going to go backpacking in July.

A. Practice the words. (CD 2 49)

1. rent a DVD tonight

2. borrow some books tomorrow

3. go backpacking in July

4. go on vacation next week

5. mail a letter this afternoon

6. read a novel this summer

B. Practice the sentence. (CD 2 50) (CD 2 51)

| He's She's | going to rent a DVD tonight. |

C. Practice the question and answer. (CD 2 52) (CD 2 53)

| When's | he / she | going to go backpacking? |
| He's / She's | | going to go backpacking in July. |

1. July

2. tomorrow

3. this evening

4. next weekend

5. on Saturday

6. after school

D. Ask and answer. (CD 2 54)

| Is | he / she | going to go on vacation tomorrow? |
| Yes, | he / she | is. | No, | he / she | isn't. |

Let's Learn More

 Where's he going to go?

 He's going to go to the barber shop.

A. Practice the words. CD 2 55

1. department store

2. barber shop

3. beauty salon

4. supermarket

5. drug store

6. gift shop

B. Practice the sentence. CD 2 56 CD 2 57

| He's She's | going to go to the department store. |

C. Practice the question and answer. CD 2 58 CD 2 59

| Where's | he | going to go? |
| | she | |

| He's | going to go to the department store. |
| She's | |

Where are they going to go?
They're going to go to the supermarket.

D. Ask and answer. CD 2 60

| Is | he | going to go to the drug store? |
| | she | |

| Yes, | he | is. | No, | he | isn't. |
| | she | | | she | |

Are they going to go to the gift shop?
Yes, they are.   No, they aren't.

Let's Build

A. Make sentences. CD 2 61

> Amy stayed home on Sunday.
> Today she is studying English.
> She's going to go to art class on Friday.

Amy's week

Sunday	Monday	Tuesday	Wednesday	Thursday	Friday	Saturday
12th	13th	14th	15th	16th	17th	18th
stay home	gymnastics	TODAY! English	shopping	math class	art class	violin practice

Ben's week

Sunday	Monday	Tuesday	Wednesday	Thursday	Friday	Saturday
12th	13th	14th	15th	16th	17th	18th
play video games	soccer practice	Today! computer class	English class	soccer practice	piano practice	play with friends

B. Ask and answer. CD 2 62

> When did Amy go to math class?
> When is Ben going to play with his friends?

Let's Read

A. Read.

Welcome to Paul's Page!

Next summer I'm going to go on a home stay. I'm going to have an American brother and sister. Their names are Joe and Linda. Two years ago, Joe stayed with my family. Now, I'm going to stay with his family for two months. I have to study English every day!

New Words

home stay
American
for two months

B. Answer the questions.

1. When is Paul going to the United States?
2. Who stayed with Paul's family?
3. What does Paul have to do now?

C. Choose the correct answer.

What does *home stay* mean?
1. stay at home with my family
2. stay away from home
3. stay with a different family

 ## Let's Start

A. Let's talk.

Hi, Andy. Jenny and I are going to go to the park. Do you want to come?

I can't.

Why not?

Because I'm sick.

What's wrong?

I have a stomachache.

That's too bad. I hope you feel better!

Thanks. Have fun at the park.

B. Let's practice. 65

| Do you want to come? | I can't. Sure! |

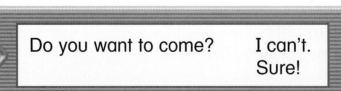

C. Practice the words. Ask and answer.

1. a cold

2. a fever

3. a headache

4. a sore throat

5. an earache

6. a stomachache

7. a toothache

8. a cough

> What's wrong?
> I have a cold.

D. Practice the grammar chant.

What's the matter with you?
You don't look very well.
   I have a toothache.
Call the dentist.
   I have a stomachache.
Call the doctor.
   I have a sore throat.
Drink some tea.
   My cold is getting worse.
Call the nurse!

Let's Learn

A. Practice the words. CD 2 69

1. write e-mail

2. paint pictures

3. collect baseball cards

4. watch sports on TV

5. surf the Internet

6. play badminton

B. Practice the sentences. CD 2 70 CD 2 71

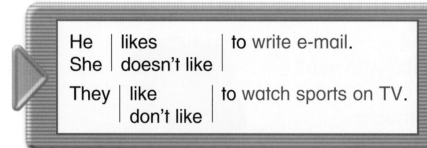

He	likes	to write e-mail.
She	doesn't like	
They	like	to watch sports on TV.
	don't like	

1.

2.

3.

C. Practice the questions and answers. CD 2 72 CD 2 73

What does	he she	like to do?	He She	likes to paint pictures.

What do they like to do?   They like to play badminton.

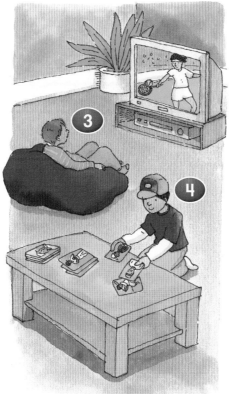

D. Ask and answer. CD 2 74

Does	he she	like to collect baseball cards?

Yes,	he she	does.	No,	he she	doesn't.

Do they like to watch sports on TV?
    Yes, they do.   No, they don't.

 What does he have to do?

He has to wash the dishes.

Let's Learn More

A. Practice the words.
 CD 2 75

1. clear the table

2. wash the dishes

3. dry the dishes

4. vacuum the carpet

5. take out the trash

6. feed the dog

B. Practice the sentences.
 CD 2 76   CD 2 77

He She	has to wash the dishes.
They have to clear the table.	

C. Practice the question and answer.

| What does | he
she | have to do? |

| He
She | has to take out the trash. |

D. What about you?

1. What do you have to do?
2. What do you like to do?

Play a game. Make sentences.

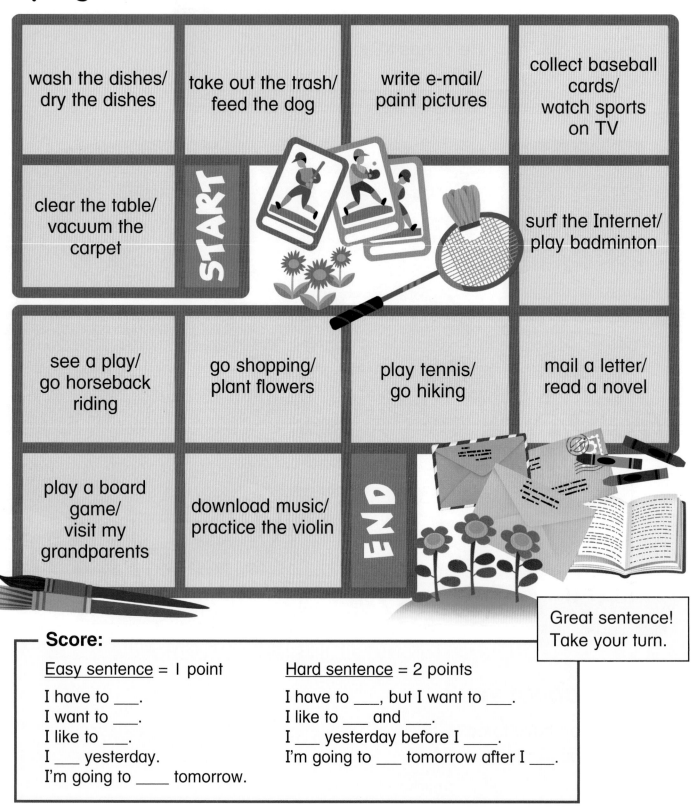

wash the dishes/
dry the dishes

take out the trash/
feed the dog

write e-mail/
paint pictures

collect baseball
cards/
watch sports
on TV

clear the table/
vacuum the
carpet

START

surf the Internet/
play badminton

see a play/
go horseback
riding

go shopping/
plant flowers

play tennis/
go hiking

mail a letter/
read a novel

play a board
game/
visit my
grandparents

download music/
practice the violin

END

Great sentence!
Take your turn.

Score:

Easy sentence = 1 point

I have to ___.
I want to ___.
I like to ___.
I ___ yesterday.
I'm going to ____ tomorrow.

Hard sentence = 2 points

I have to ___, but I want to ___.
I like to ___ and ___.
I ___ yesterday before I ____.
I'm going to ___ tomorrow after I ___.

Let's Read

A. Read. (CD 2 80)

What Are You Like?

1. You want to play a video game.
   You have to do your homework.
   - A. I'm going to do my homework.
   - B. I'm going to play a video game.

2. You have a test tomorrow.
   - A. I'm going to study.
   - B. I'm going to watch TV.

3. You have some money.
   - A. I'm going to save it.
   - B. I'm going to spend it.

Answers
All A: You are very serious. Have a little more fun!
2 A and 1 B: You are serious, but you like to have fun, too.
2 B and 1 A: You are easygoing, but you can be serious, too.
All B: You are very easygoing. Be a little more serious!

New Words

save
spend
serious
easygoing

B. What about you?

What kind of person are you? Are you a serious person or an easygoing person?

C. Choose the best answer.

Choose the best answers for the questions.

1. What are you like?
   A. I'm easygoing.
   B. I have brown hair.

2. What do you look like?
   A. I'm serious.
   B. I have blue eyes.

Listen and circle. CD 2 81

1.

2.

3.

4.

5.

6.

CHRIS AND CINDY'S TREASURE HUNT

Part Four

A. Read. CD 2 82

"Carlsbad Caverns is so big," said Chris. "I feel so small."

"There's a box," said Cindy. "Let's look inside."

"It's a scrapbook," said Cindy.

"Look! We're riding on a camel in Egypt," said Chris.

"And we're standing in front of the waterfall at Iguazu Falls," said Cindy.

"Thank you, Aunt Angie," said Chris. "This is a great treasure."

"I'm glad you like it," said Aunt Angie.

"Why are there blank pages in the scrapbook?" asked Cindy.

"Because we're going to have more adventures!" said Aunt Angie.

B. What about you?

1. Do you have a scrapbook?
2. Where in the world do you want to go?
3. What do you want to see?

New Words	
Carlsbad Caverns	blank
scrapbook	adventures
camel	

Let's Go 4 Syllabus

Unit 1   Birthdays

Let's Start	**Let's Learn**	**Let's Learn More**	**Let's Build**
When's your birthday? It's on August 3rd. Asking about and stating the date Asking about and stating birthdays What's the date today? It's the 21st. Asking about and stating the date	He had a party yesterday. She didn't drink hot chocolate yesterday. Stating what someone did or did not do What did he do yesterday? He took a test. Did she fly a kite yesterday? Yes, she did. No, she didn't. Asking questions with simple past irregular verbs Asking what someone did	He/She/They won a race. He/She/They didn't find any money. What happened? He/She/They found some money. Asking about and stating what happened	I met a movie star on the 13th. When did he fly a kite? He flew a kite on Sunday the 20th. Asking about and answering what happened and when **Let's Read** Welcome to Abby's Page

Unit 2   The Great Outdoors

Let's Start	**Let's Learn**	**Let's Learn More**	**Let's Build**
The school trip is tomorrow. I'm really excited! Me, too! Talking about what is going to happen What's the weather going to be like tomorrow? It's going to be cold. Talking about what the weather is going to be like	He's going to go to the mountains. She's going to go to the beach. Talking about where people are going to go He should take sunscreen. He shouldn't take a tent. Should he/she/they take sunscreen? Yes, he/she/they should. No, he/she//they shouldn't. What else should he/she/they take? He/She/They should take a camera. Asking for and giving advice	He has a mitt and a bat. He doesn't have a fishing rod or a bucket. He's probably going to play baseball. What's she going to do? She's probably going to go hiking. What are they going to do? They're probably going to play baseball. Asking and stating what someone may do	He has sunscreen. He's probably going to go to the beach. She wants a cat. She's probably going to go to the pet store. They have a kite. They're probably going to go to the park. Where's she going to go? She's probably going to go to the library. Where are they going to go? They're probably going to go to the park. Asking and stating where someone may go **Let's Read** How to Make a Rainbow

Units 1–2 Listen and Review   **Let's Read About Chris and Cindy Part One**

Unit 3   Hopes and Dreams

Let's Start	Let's Learn	Let's Learn More	Let's Build
What do you want to be? I want to be an astronaut. Do you want to be a singer? Yes, I do. / No, I don't. *Asking about future professions*	He/She wants to be a flight attendant. He/She doesn't want to be a delivery person. What does he/she want to be? He/She wants to be a truck driver. Does he/she want to be a delivery person? Yes, he/she does. No, he/she doesn't. *Asking about and stating and stating future professions*	He/She wants to climb a mountain. He/She doesn't want to build a house. What does he/she want to do? He/She wants to design a video game. Does she want to build a house? Yes, she does. No, she doesn't. *Asking about and expressing desires*	I want to ___, but I don't want to _____. *Expressing desires* **Let's Read** Anna and Teri Johnson, Volunteer Sisters

Unit 4   School

Let's Start	Let's Learn	Let's Learn More	Let's Build
Why do you like science? I think it's easy. What's your favorite subject? I like history. *Eliciting and expressing personal opinions* *Comparing school subjects*	The orange bottle is bigger than the blue bottle. The green bottle is the biggest. Which pencil is the longest? The yellow pencil is the longest. Which pencil is the shortest? The red pencil is the shortest. Is the green pencil the longest? Yes, it is. / No, it isn't. *Comparing objects that are alike*	Matt's pie is good. Who's the best /worst swimmer? Ryan is the best. Kevin is the worst. Is Kevin a better runner than Ann? Yes, he is. / No, he isn't. Is Kevin the best swimmer? Yes, he is. / No, he isn't. *Comparing abilities*	The police car is heavier than the motorcycle. The fire engine is the heaviest. *Comparing objects that are not alike* **Let's Read** Which One Is the Fastest?

Units 3–4 Listen and Review   Let's Read About Chris and Cindy Part Two

Unit 5   Indoors and Outdoors

Let's Start	Let's Learn	Let's Learn More	Let's Build
Can you wait for us? Sure, no problem! Sorry, I can't. *Requesting that someone wait* He's/She's surprised. *Describing people's feelings*	He/She practiced the violin. He/She didn't download music. What did he do yesterday? He practiced the violin. What did they do yesterday? They visited their grandparents. Did he listen to the radio? Yes, he did. No, he didn't. Did they play a board game? Yes, they did. No, they didn't. *Asking and stating what someone did*	He/She/They went under a bridge and up a hill. Where did the boy/girl go? He went over the wall. She went through the tunnel. *Describing where people went*	Where did Ken/Stacy go? Who did he/she go with? What did he/she do? What did he/she eat? When did he/she go? *Answering questions with details* **Let's Read** Aunt Tina's Trip

Unit 6 People

Let's Start
Can I help you?
Yes, thanks.
No, thanks. I'm OK.
Offering someone help

Who are you looking for?
I'm looking for my aunt.
Identifying family members

Let's Learn
He has short red hair and green eyes.

What does his cousin look like?
His cousin has brown hair and blue eyes.
Describing people's eye color, hair color, and hair style

Let's Learn More
The boy is wearing glasses.

Which boy is Brian's older brother?
He's the boy with curly brown hair and brown eyes.
He's the boy in shorts and a blue, striped shirt.
Identifying people by appearance

Let's Build
Identifying people by appearance

Let's Read
Let's Make Fingerprints

Units 5–6 Listen and Review   Let's Read About Chris and Cindy Part Three

Unit 7 Future Plans

Let's Start
Are you going to do anything this weekend?
Yes, I am. I'm going to see my cousin.
No, I'm not. I'm going to stay home.

What's he/she going to do?
He's/She's going to go shopping.
What are they going to do?
They're going to play ice hockey.
Asking and stating what people are going to do

Let's Learn
He's going to rent a DVD tonight.

When's he/she going to go backpacking?
He's/She's going to go backpacking in July.

Is he going to go on vacation tomorrow?
Yes, he is.
No, he isn't.
Asking and stating what people are going to do and when

Let's Learn More
He's going to go to the department store.

Where's he going to go?
He's going to go to the department store.
Where are they going to go?
They're going to go to the supermarket.

Is he going to go to the drug store?
Yes, he is. / No, he isn't.
Are they going to go to the gift shop?
Yes, they are. / No, they aren't.
Asking and answering about where someone is going

Let's Build
Amy stayed home on Sunday.
Today she is studying English.
She's going to go to art class on Friday.

When did Amy go to math class?
When is Ben going to play with his friends?
Asking and stating what people do and when

Let's Read
Welcome to Paul's Page!

Unit 8 Work and Play

Let's Start
Do you want to come?
I can't.
Sure!
Making an invitation

What's wrong?
I have a cold.
Asking and answering about illnesses

Let's Learn
He/she likes/doesn't like to write e-mail.
They like/don't like to watch sports on TV.

What does he/she like to do?
He/She likes to paint pictures.
What do they like to do?
They like to play badminton.

Does he/she like to collect baseball cards? Yes, he/she does. / No, he/she doesn't.

Do they like to watch sports on TV? Yes, they do. / No, they don't.
Expressing likes and dislikes

Let's Learn More
He/She has to wash the dishes.
They have to clear the table.

What does he/she have to do?
He/she has to take out the trash.
Asking and stating what someone has to do

Let's Build
Talking about wants, needs, and likes

Let's Read
What Are You Like? Quiz

Units 7–8 Listen and Review   Let's Read About Chris and Cindy Part Four

Word List

A

a 4
a little more 71
about 20
adventure 73
after 59
afternoon 58
ago 2
air 35
airplane 19
all 34
always 55
am 56
Amazon 73
American 63
amusement park 44
an 9
and 9
any 6
animals 27
answers 71
anything 56
anywhere 47
apple 26
architect 22
are 15
aren't 61
arm 8
around 24
art class 62
asked 37
astronaut 9
at 8
ate 6
August 2
aunt 47
aunt's 2
Australia 45
away 53

B

backpacking 58
bad 32
badminton 66
bag 30
bakery 16
bangs 48
barber shop 60
baseball 14
baseball cap 50
baseball cards 66
baseball game 40
bat 14
bath 26
be 3
beach 12
beard 48
beautiful 47
beauty salon 60
because 28
before 7
best 28
better 32
bicycle 14
big 19
bigger 30
biggest 30
birthday 2

black 47
blank 73
blond 48
blouse 50
blue 30
board game 40
boat 24
book 16
books 58
bookstore 16
bored 39
borrow 58
bottle 30
box 30
boy 43
break 6
breakfast 9
bridge 42
broke 6
brother 49
brown 48
brush (v) 53
bucket 14
build 24
but 19
buy 57
by 35

C

call 65
came 7
camel 73
camera 13
can 17
can't 47
candles 9
car 24
Carlsbad Caverns 73
carpet 68
castle 55
cave 55
cell phone 6
cheetah 34
chocolate 4
chopsticks 26
class 62
clear 68
climb 24
clue 19
coin 34
cold (adj) 10
cold (n) 65
collect 66
color 48
come 64
come on 21
computer class 62
cook (n) 33
cook (v) 26
cool 11
cough 65
cousin 47
crocodile 45
curly 48

D

dad 47
dance 21

dancer 21
dark 55
date 2
day 7
dear 45
delivery person 22
dentist 65
department store 60
desert 55
design (v) 24
did 5
didn't 2
different 53
dinner 26
dishes 68
do 5
doctor 65
does 23
doesn't 14
dog 26
doing 52
dolphin 27
don't 10
down 42
download 40
drank 4
dreams 20
drink 4
drive 24
drives 27
drug store 60
dry 68
duck 35
DVD 58

E

earache 65
easier 28
easy 28
easy-going 71
eat 6
eating 52
Egypt 37
elephants 34
else 13
e-mail 66
embarrassed 39
English 26
evening 59
ever 34
every 27
everyone 46
excited 10
eyes 46

F

face 48
falcon 35
family 63
fast 35
faster 34
fastest 34
father 47
father's 2
favorite 28
fed 45
feed 26

feeds 27
feel 64
fever 65
fight 34
find 6
finger 53
fingerprint 53
fire engine 34
first 7
fishing 15
fishing rod 14
flashlight 12
flew 4
flight attendant 22
flowers 57
fly 4
foggy 11
for 9
found 6
french fries 44
Friday 3
friend 49
from 51
front 19
fun 9
future 56

G

game 40
gave 39
geography 29
get 6
getting 65
gift shop 60
girl 43
glad 73
glass 17
glasses 50
go 4
going 3
good 32
got 6
grandfather 47
grandma 47
grandmother 47
grandpa 47
grandparents 40
gray 48
great 9
Great Pyramid 37
green 30
gymnastics 62

H

had 4
hair 46
hairbrush 34
hands 53
happened 7
happy 2
hard 28
harder 37
has 14
hat 12
have 4
having 45
he 4

he's 12
headache 65
heavier 31
heaviest 31
heavy 31
held 45
helmet 14
help 27
helps 27
her 46
here 37
here's 55
hi 37
hiking 15
hill 42
hills 57
his 6
history 29
hold 45
holding 19
home 9
home stay 63
homework 26
hope 56
hopes 20
horse 35
horseback riding 57
hospital 27
hot 11
hot chocolate 4
house 24
how 9
humid 11
hunt 19
hurry 38

I

I 2
I'm 10
ice hockey 56
idea 21
Iguazu Falls 55
in 7
in front of 17
indoors 17
inside 17
interested 39
Internet 66
into 42
is 2
isn't 10
it 3
it's 2

J

jackets 10
January 3
jeans 51
July 58
jump rope 34

K

kangaroo 45
key 34
kids 37
kind 71

kite 4
know 2
koala 45
kph (kilometers per hour) 35

L

land 35
learn 58
let's 21
letter 58
library 16
lift 53
light 31
lighter 31
lightest 31
lights 17
like 10
likes 27
line 38
lion 35
lions 34
listen 26
listened 40
literature 29
little 71
live 35
long 31
longer 31
longest 31
look 35
looked 45
looking 46
lose 6
lost 6
lot 9
lotion 53
luck 56

M

magic trick 26
mail 58
make 17
man 51
March 3
math class 62
matter 47
May 3
me 10
mean 63
meet 4
met 4
mitt 14
mom 47
Monday 3
money 6
months 63
more 71
morning 27
mother 47
motorcycle 34
mountain 24
mountains 12
moustache 48
move 35
movie star 4
much 6